For Naomi, Joe, Eddie,
Laura and Geraldine
M.R.

First published 1987 by
Walker Books Ltd
87 Vauxhall Walk
London SE11 5HJ

This edition published 2000

2 4 6 8 10 9 7 5 3 1

Text © 1987 Michael Rosen
Illustrations © 1987 Quentin Blake

This book has been typeset in Trump Mediæval.

Printed in Hong Kong

British Library Cataloguing in Publication Data
A catalogue record for this book is
available from the British Library.

ISBN 0-7445-7764-0

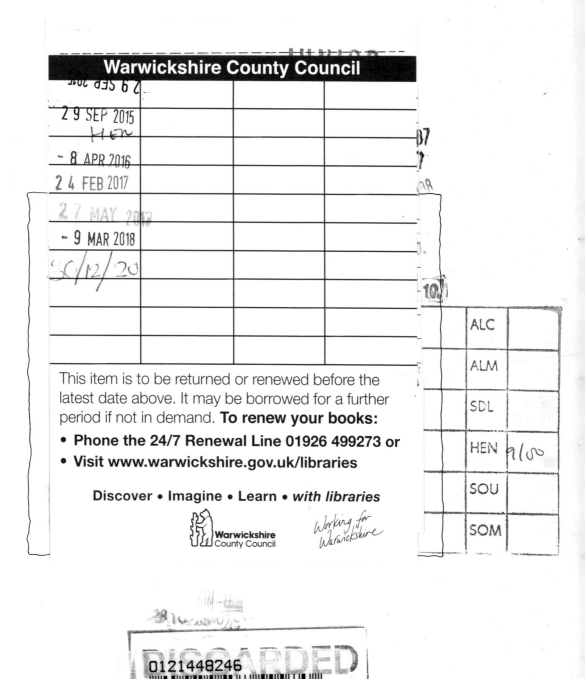

Warwickshire County Council

2 9 SEP 2015			
HEN			
- 8 APR 2016			
2 4 FEB 2017			
2 7 MAY 2017			
- 9 MAR 2018			
30/12/20			

This item is to be returned or renewed before the
latest date above. It may be borrowed for a further
period if not in demand. **To renew your books:**

- **Phone the 24/7 Renewal Line 01926 499273 or**
- **Visit www.warwickshire.gov.uk/libraries**

Discover • Imagine • Learn • *with libraries*

Warwickshire County Council

Working for Warwickshire

ALC	
ALM	
SDL	
HEN	9/00
SOU	
SOM	

MICHAEL ROSEN
ILLUSTRATED BY
QUENTIN BLAKE

Hard-boiled Legs
The Breakfast Book

WALKER BOOKS
AND SUBSIDIARIES
LONDON • BOSTON • SYDNEY

Breakfast Time

Someone's dropped a bottle of milk,
the dustman's dropped a dustbin.
Someone's found a piece of potato in their shoe,
the baby's eating a sock.
When is it?
Breakfast time.

The cat's on the table eating someone's bacon,
someone's wiped butter on their trousers.
Someone's poured tea into the sugar bowl,
the baby is eating eggshells.
When is it?
Breakfast time.

Someone thinks they're going to get very angry,
someone thinks they're going crazy.
Someone thinks they're going to scream,
the baby has tipped cornflakes over its head.
When is it?
Breakfast time.

What If...

What if
a piece of toast turned into a piece of ghost
just as you were eating it
and you thought you were going to sink your
teeth into a lovely crunchy piece of hot toast
and butter and instead this cold wet feeling
jumps into your mouth
going,
"Whooooooooooooooooooooo!"
right down into your stomach

and your mum says,
"What did you say?"
You say, "Nothing, Mum,"
but the ghost sitting in your stomach
does it again.
"Whoooooooooooooooooooo!"
and everyone looks at you.

Things We Say

A Little Boy Came
Down to Breakfast

A little boy came down to breakfast
with bananas stuck in his ears.

Everyone said hello to him
but he didn't take any notice.
So his mum said, "Are you all right?"
but the little boy said nothing.
So his sister said, "Are you all right?"
but the little boy still said nothing.

Then his brother noticed that he had bananas stuck in his ears, so he said, "Hey, you've got bananas stuck in your ears," and the little boy said, "What?" So his brother said it again. "You've got bananas stuck in your ears," and the little boy said, "What?" So the brother shouted really loudly at him, "YOU'VE GOT BANANAS STUCK IN YOUR EARS!" And the little boy shouted back, "I'M SORRY, I CAN'T HEAR YOU. I'VE GOT BANANAS IN MY EARS!"

Nat and Anna

Nat and Anna were having breakfast.
Mum said to Anna, "I'm just going upstairs
to get ready. Make sure Nat finishes his
breakfast, will you?"

Mum went out.
Nat got off his chair.
Anna said, "Sit down, Nat."
Nat said, "I'm going for a walk."
Anna said, "Sit down, Nat."
Nat came back and sat down.
Nat said, "I sat down, Anna. Can I get up now?"
Anna said, "Sit down, Nat."
Nat said, "I'm going to the beach."
Anna said, "Sit down, Nat."

Nat went under the table and sat down.
Nat said, "I'm sitting down now, Anna."
Anna said, "You can't sit there, Nat."
Nat said, "I'm having a picnic at the beach."
Anna said, "But you haven't got a picnic with you."
Nat came out from under the table and sat down on his chair.

Mum shouted from upstairs, "Are you all right?"
Anna said, "Yes."

Nat got off the chair with a bowl of cornflakes.
Anna said, "What are you doing?"
Nat said, "I'm going to the beach with a picnic."
Anna said, "Sit down, Nat."

Nat got under the table and sat down with a
bowl of cornflakes.

Nat said, "I'm sitting down having my picnic
at the beach."

Anna said, "I'm going to pull you out of there,
Nat."

Nat said, "You can't. You're not on the beach."

Anna said, "I can. Look."

Anna pulled Nat very hard.

The cornflakes and milk spilt all over the floor.

Mum shouted from upstairs,
"Everything all right?"

Nat said, "No."

Anna said, "You're going to get into trouble
now, Nat."

Mum came in.

Mum said, "What is going on? What's all this mess all over the floor?"

Nat said, "We're having a picnic at the beach, aren't we, Anna?"

Mum said, "Listen here, Anna. Next time I leave you alone like that, don't get Nat playing your silly games, do you understand? Now go to your room and stay there."

Anna walked out.

Nat said, "Can I go with her?"

Mum said, "No."

Anna said, "No no no no no no no no no no no."

Nat said, "Why's Anna shouting?"

What Happens Next?

If he treads on the dog…
If the dog tries to run…
If the table moves…
If the parrot…
If the man up the ladder…
OH NO! OH NO! OH NO!

What If…

What if
hard-boiled eggs turned into hard-boiled legs
just when your dad was eating his egg
and he says,
"Hey, what's this?"
and the hard-boiled leg starts to run all round
the table and your dad starts to chase it.
"I want my egg!"
but the leg stands up and says,
    "You can't catch me,
     I'm no egg.
     You can't catch me,
     I'm a hard-boiled leg,"

and it runs out the door and your dad runs out
the door after it,
still wearing his pyjamas.

WALKER BOOKS

Hard-boiled Legs

MICHAEL ROSEN says, "What a clever fellow Quentin Blake is! I came to Walker Books one day and Quentin was sitting there with a scrappy piece of paper. On it was written a list of ideas: jokes, riddles, conversations, poems, things to do, cartoons … and that's how these books (pictured below) came about. When I was a kid one of my favourite books was *The News Chronicle I-Spy Annual*. It would last me the whole year. I hope my series does the same for kids today."

Michael Rosen is one of the most popular contemporary poets and authors of books for children. His titles include *We're Going on a Bear Hunt* (Winner of the Smarties Book Prize), *This Is Our House* and *Little Rabbit Foo Foo*. He also compiled *Classic Poetry: An Illustrated Collection*. He's a regular broadcaster on BBC Radio and in 1997 received the Eleanor Farjeon Award for services to children's literature. Michael Rosen lives with his family in London.

QUENTIN BLAKE says, "I have always liked Michael Rosen's poems; and what I particularly enjoy when I am illustrating them is that he seems to know everything about everyday life, but at the same time there is some fantasy that gets in as well."

Quentin Blake consistently tops all polls as the most popular children's book artist. The illustrator of numerous Roald Dahl titles and several Michael Rosen poetry collections, he has also created many acclaimed picture books of his own, including *Mr Magnolia* (Winner of the Kate Greenaway Medal), *The Green Ship* and *Zagazoo*. In 1999 he was appointed the first Children's Laureate. He lives in London.

ISBN 0-7445-7764-0 (pb)   ISBN 0-7445-7765-9 (pb)   ISBN 0-7445-7763-2 (pb)   ISBN 0-7445-7766-7 (pb)